Down Rainbow Road
New & Selected Poems

Rob Wallis's fifth collection of poetry, *Caught Jesting*, was published by Birdfish Books. His poems have appeared in various magazines and anthologies both in Australia and overseas. He has won the John Shaw Neilson Poetry Award, the W. B. Yeats Poetry Prize, and has twice won the MPU International Poetry Competition's Martin Downey Urban Realist Award. He has been shortlisted twice for the Fish Publishing International Poetry Competition, Dublin, the Bridport Prize, UK, and the ACU Prize for Poetry. Rob lives in Castlemaine, Victoria.

Down Rainbow Road
New & Selected Poems

ℭℬ

Rob Wallis

Foreword by Maria Millers

Clouds of Magellan Press

The poetry sequences *Inheritance* and *Muscular Flirtations* are published here for the first time by Clouds of Magellan Press. The poems in *Selected Poems* were previously published in the following books and are reprinted here by kind permission of the publishers:

The Match Of The Hunter (1998 Woorilla Publications); *My Life As A Sheep Dog* (2009 Mark Time Books); *Man In A Glass Suit* (2011 Mark Time Books); *An Elegant Sufficiency* (2015 Birdfish Books); *Caught Jesting* (2018 Birdfish Books).

Clouds of Magellan Press
www.cloudsofmagellanpress.net

ISBN: (paperback) 978-0-9874037-7-3

Cover design and layout: Gordon Thompson
Cover image: Guy James Whitworth – www.guyjameswhitworth.com

Distribution by eBook Alchemy
www.ebookalchemy.com

For Wim, again, and The Alluvians

Contents

Selected Poems

from *The Match Of The Hunter*

from *My Life As A Sheep Dog*

from *Man In A Glass Suit*

from *An Elegant Sufficiency*

from *Caught Jesting*

Acknowledgements

Many thanks to the publishers of my earlier collections who kindly gave their permission for the reprinting of previously published poems: Maria Millers of Woorilla Publications (*The Match Of The Hunter*), Ross Donlon of Mark Time Books (*My Life As A Sheep Dog, Man In A Glass Suit*) and Tegan Gigante of Birdfish Books (*An Elegant Sufficiency, Caught Jesting*).

'asleep in my arms' was previously published in *Love from a Distance: bent street*, 4.1, and 'Percy Haynes Has a Rare Win' and 'A Policeman's Report' in *Kiss my Apocalypse: bent street* 4.2 (Clouds of Magellan Press, Melbourne 2020). 'Gay Bar' was published in *Bold. Stories from older lesbian, gay, bisexual, transgender & intersex people*, editor David Hardy (The Rag & Bone Man Press).

I would like to acknowledge the contribution of Castlemaine's Thursday afternoon poetry group where some of these poems were workshopped.

I would also like to thank the Australian Lesbian and Gay Archives for their invaluable assistance when I was researching the poems in *Inheritance*.

Finally, I wish to thank my publisher Gordon Thompson for his professional expertise and support, and Guy James Whitworth for allowing us to use one of his wonderful watercolours on the jacket.

RW

Foreword

To read Rob Wallis's *Down Rainbow Road: New & Selected Poems* is to enter into a life that for many may not be their lived experience; but this does not in any way diminish the universal and shared aspects of this collection: the need for love, intimacy and acceptance.

To read about the bigotry, cruelties, injustices and hypocrisies of past and not-so-past generations, told for the first time in the conciseness of poetic form is uncomfortably confronting and a reminder that prejudices still exist today.

Here we have the poetry of a man responding to a world where difference was marginalised; responding sometimes with pain, sometimes with pleasure, but always with honesty: personal experiences from an early awareness and distress about his own sexuality to a growing acceptance and finally to finding mature love.

There is an honesty in the retelling of this early awareness of 'difference' and what it takes to avoid exclusion by suppressing his true self:

> *As a young man I lived*
> *in someone else's country, too afraid*
> *to give my difference a name.*

So many instances of perceived difference; yet some of these feelings of youthful uncertainties is where readers, gay or straight, would find common ground.

This is poetry of experience rather than ideas, and the experience is often presented without comment, the words of description supplying the emotion – moral observations without the moralizing.

In the final section of the book there is a return to poetry published earlier and here we find the poet at word play and 'piss taking' as he delights in pricking the pomposity of politically correct weasel words and human behavior generally.

Maria Millers
Founder of the Woorilla Poetry Prize

Inheritance

Inheritance, an exploration of the history of gay men in Australia, was never intended to be a comprehensive coverage, rather it's a sample of events, experiences, emotions over the past four centuries. Research proved difficult, at times shocking. So much of our history has been ignored, covered up, repressed. Much of the material came from newspaper reports of court convictions, and is often negative and judgemental. I wanted to capture the voices of the men involved, judges, 'felons', survivors, using their language, words that had the power to denounce, denigrate, and liberate. It was a relief to find a few triumphs, Percy Haynes, Claudio Arrau and, most significantly, the 2016 Victorian State Government Apology. Addressing our past reminds us of the gains we've made, and gives us a voice for the challenges still ahead.

RW

After the Shipwreck

1727

Two sailors, boys,
Adriaen Spoor and Pieter Engels,
survivors of the 'Zeewijk'
wrecked off the coast
of Western Australia,
were caught by crewmen in
the abominable
and God forsaken deeds
of Sodom and Gomorrah.

And given death sentences,
the ship's crew
judge, jury and executioner.

How do you put that
into practice
on a remote island?
Easy. You maroon them
on two rocky outcrops
until they starve to death.

The New Zealand Solution

1796

I, Governor Arthur Phillip,
firmly believe
that only two offences
deserve the death penalty,
murder and sodomy.

When the first case of sodomy
came before me
I did not put this belief
into practice. Instead
I offered an alternative,
in the hope
that the dread of this
would operate much stronger
than the fear of death.

My solution: to imprison
the convicted felon
until the opportunity offered
to deliver him
to the natives of New Zealand
and let them eat him.

Class Act

1828

In the first ever
recorded execution
for a homosexual act,
a court in Sydney
ordered two men,
Alexander Brown
and Richard Lister,
to hang by the neck.

Lister, a crewman
on the whaling ship
'Royal Sovereign',
received a last minute
reprieve. Brown,
the ship's first officer,
was duly hanged.

Judgement

1835

Convict Edmund Carmen,
you were arrested
by the police
near Wollongong
dressed in a woman's
gown and cape...

You will be sent
back to Sydney
with the proviso
that you will not
be assigned again
to this district.

I find you guilty
of improper conduct
and sentence you
to 150 lashes.

Newspaper reports agreed:

unnatural crime abominable
            behaviour depraved
            act of disgusting conduct
                atrocity of the most
shocking odious character

Men Scrambling

1838

The Select Committee
        on Transportation
and its Influence
        on the Moral State
of Society in the Colonies

reported
        its concerns
on Doors being Opened
        Men Scrambling
into their Own Beds
        from Others
in a Hurried Manner
        Concealment
being their Object

Upwards of 100
        as Many as 150
Couples can be
        Pointed Out
Half with Names like
        Kitty   Sally
Nancy   Polly   Bet

who Habitually Associate
        for the Most
Detestable Intercourse

Moral Perception
        so Completely Absorbed
they are Said To Be
        Married
Man and Wife

Letter To Jack

Found in the possession of a male convict hanged in 1846

Dear Lover,

I hope you wont forget me

when my bones are moulded away

your precious sight

was always a welcome

and loving charming spectacle

I value death

but it is leaving you my dear

no one to look after you

the only thing that grieves me love

is when i think of the pleasant nights

we had together

I hope you wont

fall in love

with no other man

when I am dead

I remain your true and loving

affectionate Lover

Having It Both Ways

Sailor, 1853

buggery is fine
        on board ship
just fine   buggery
        there are no women
on board ship
        so   what do you expect

but on dry land
        buggers should be shot
there are women
        on dry land
so buggers   should be shot
        shot   shot

Romantic Friendship

1859

I, Robert Herbert,
as the first
Colonial Secretary of Queensland,
am rarely apart
from my Attorney General
John Bramston.
We have shared
a grand house and gardens
'Herston'
for many years.

We write love letters
to each other
and pose for portraits,
holding hands
or embracing.

When people ask me
why I'm a lifelong bachelor
I always reply:
It does not seem to be reasonable
to tell a man
who is happy and content,
to marry a woman
who may turn out to be
a great disappointment.

Breaking His Neck

1863

The last homosexual
to be executed
was hanged in Tasmania.

Hendrik Witnalder,
a black South African convict,
was charged with sodomy,
along with a 14 year-old boy
who was later released.

How do you hang someone
of *tiny stature?*

You tie weights
to his feet
in case his body
is too light
to break his neck.

Captain Moonlight

we met in prison
and were soon friends

after our release
we were complicit

in crime   he was shot
dead   died in my arms

my dearest friend
we were one

in heart and soul
one heart   one soul

I wept over him
like a child

laid his head
upon my breast

and farewelled him
with a kiss

I long to join him
in the grave

where there will be
no more parting

*Two Friends Reunited in Death: this epitaph was written in 1879 by
the bushranger Captain Moonlight (Andrew George Scott) who wanted
to be buried with his presumed lover James Nesbit. After he was
hanged his wish was denied. They are now buried together in the
Gundagai cemetery.*

Inverts According To Forel

Auguste Forel, The Sexual Question, *1908*

Some of us may still qualify
for Forel's description of male inverts,
have *the same feelings as girls towards boys,*
fond of religious forms and ceremonies,
admire luxurious apartments,
but I doubt if this applies to us all.
We may be guilty of not being
constant in our love
and inclined to polyandry,
the candy shop was closed
for so many years. Many of us
could be described as *well-conducted inverts*
who possess the most delicate sentiment
yet it's regrettable that some still *become pessimists*
owing to the shame and the grief.
Inverts of this class may commit suicide
if they see it as *a struggle against*
a morbid appetite, prefer death to defeat
which they consider a dishonour.

We'd all be happy to agree
that our *ideal is to obtain*
a legal licence for marriage between men,
Forel's prescient notion ahead of his time.
But few would now see homosexual love
as *pathological by nature,*
nor view ourselves as *psychopaths*
or neurotics whose sexual appetite
is not only abnormal but usually exalted.
Exalted? Lofty, noble, elated?
Let's go with that.

The Truth Will Out

Headlines from the Melbourne Truth, *1914-1920*

A Doddering Degenerate

A Grave, Glaring, Growing Evil

Alleged Offences Against a Boy

Amorous Antics of an Advertising Actor

Degenerate 'Dressed Up Like A Doll'

Dirty Degenerate Dungeoned

Disgusting Doings of a Degenerate

Disgusting Depravity

Feculent Farrington

Filthy Fellow Fined a Fiver

Filthy Fellow Parades as Flash French Floosie

Filthy Old Fellow Fined Again

Grinning Grimacer's Games in the Garden

How Nuss Nussed the Naughty Ninny

Mugged and Maimed by Amorous Males

Park Pest Tries Pranks on a Policeman

Park Pest Sent to Prison

Pervert Pearson's Putrid Practices

Pestilent Perverts

Pornic Pranks in Public Gardens

Powdered and Painted Perverts

Queer Queans

Revolting Rumours Regarding a Religious Man

Salvation Army Sergeant's Sin

Shameful Stories of Salicity

Shocking Stories of Boy Scouts

Soldier Sergeant Severely Sentenced

The Potting of a 'Pretty Joey'

Teacher's Terrible Turpitude

Dennis Dunn Does His Duty

1921

A city businessman, I take my civic duties
seriously. Hence my outrage when I came
across a seaman masturbating in the toilets
of the Bijou Theatre Arcade in Bourke Street.
The impudent fellow even had the cheek
to suggest a mutual tug. That's the reason why
I followed the pervert to the Eastern Markets
and back to the Bijou, collecting a policeman
along the way. You can imagine my satisfaction
when we caught the odious beast in a cubicle
with a printer's assistant, up to his old tricks.
He received a six months prison sentence.

Excuses, Excuses

1925

What did wharf labourer James Gore
think he was doing in the darkened doorway
of a warehouse in Bright's Lane,
his trousers around his knees,
his person in the fundament
of Selwyn Lindsay, an actor?

In court he denied any wrongdoing.
Said he'd stepped into the doorway
to answer a call of nature.
Lindsay also denied guilt,
he went there to adjust
recently purchased braces
that were too tight.
Both claimed to be unaware
of the other's presence
until a night watchman
shone his electric torch on them.

A powder puff and rouge,
part of his professional kit,
found in Lindsay's pocket,
clinched the watchman's version.
The jury found them guilty.
They were both sentenced
to fifteen months hard labour in Pentridge.

Shoeshine

1926

Eighteen-year-old Earnest Pollard
told the court
he went to the Austral Cafe
in Exhibition Street
to have his shoes shined.

Resident shoeshine Fred Lee
took him to a back room,
knelt down before him
and brushed his trousers.
Next he ripped open his fly,
grabbed his hands
and pushed him against a table.
Lee then started to suck his penis.
Pollard said, *Let me go,*
but Lee only laughed
and kept on sucking.
He finally let Pollard go
after *I spent in his mouth.*

Pollard left the shop and told
the first Constable he saw
what had happened.

Fred went to Pentridge
for three months.
His regulars missed him.

A Taxi Driver Tells The Police

1927

I was standing by my yellow cab
at the Princes Bridge station taxi rank
when a man turned up
and started a conversation. He noticed
the bulge in my front fly
when I pressed up against him.
That's when he asked me
to drive him home. I stopped
on the road through the Domain.
He paid too much then suggested
I join him on the back seat.
He unbuttoned the front
of my trousers, unbuttoned
his trousers at the back, pulled
them down, caught hold
of my penis and started to rub
his hand up and down
until I got an erection.
Oh what a beaut! he said.
The best I ever felt.
I got behind him
and he guided my penis
into his backside, at the same time
saying, *Oh, it's lovely.* Then
I began to push my penis
back and forward in his back passage.
Then the Constable arrived.

Stan Clarke, taxi driver, received a three months sentence.
Russell Luke, Myer's department manager, got six months.

Percy Haynes Has A Rare Win

1935

Dressed as a woman
because it made me
feel good about myself,
and anything for a lark,
I went window shopping
in Melbourne
then went to the pictures.

Oh the romance
of being Ginger Rogers
as the dashing Fred Astaire
swept me around the dance floor
in 'Top Hat'.

Ever on the alert
two detectives followed me
home on the tram
and arrested me
at the gate
in front of the neighbours.
The judge, bless him,
threw the case out.
If a woman, he argued,
could wear jodhpurs,
he saw no reason
why a man
couldn't wear a dress.
I could have kissed him.

A Policeman's Report

1939

Usually we don't know the person
whose done themself in,
but this one was different.
Turns out that this bloke
was Jack Dale, the famous
American singer and composer.
We found him dead
in a St. Kilda flat, a suicide note
next to the body.
To whom it may concern
it began, then he mentioned
the three people in his life
who mattered the most, who he'd lost
to death,
to marriage,
to his own unfaithfulness.
But no names, no pronouns.
Without these people, he said,
I have nothing to live for.

'Truth' had a field day.
*70 Pound A Week Star Whistler's
Queer Note Before End.*
Readers knew what they meant.

Interpreting Truth

Perverts in the Ti-Tree (Melbourne Truth *headline)*

Ah the ti-tree,
childhood's summer track
through its stunted foliage
where we dragged
umbrella and towels,
buckets and spades,
hopping over the hot sand
like excited wallabies
if we took our sandals off
before we reached
the soothing flat
wetness of the sea.

Little did we know
that in this scented arbour
lurked the perverts,
hanging from branches
like fat sweaty spiders
waiting to pounce,
to cocoon us
in the threads of their filth,
their deviant desires,
to probe our soft sunburnt skin
with their sticky feelers
and slowly, slowly eat us.

Kamp

During World War Two
fifteen American soldiers
drove six Australian *girls*
into the lush New Guinea bush.
They had *situational sex*,
men *making do*
because there were no women.
Butch men
having sex with *queens*
meant they didn't lose
their masculine status,
they were having sex
with females.
It also meant
they could return home
after the war was over
to their wives or girlfriends
as if nothing had happened.

A Question of Morale

During World War Two
it was widely believed
that homosexuals in the services
would destroy morale
and be useless soldiers.

Dudly Cave overheard
two soldiers
talking about him.
He's a nancy boy,
one said. *He can't be,*
the other replied,
he was terribly brave in action.

Peanutting

1957

was when you stole into a toilet
and a young
cute and cuddly man
winked at you, gave you
a knowing come-hither look
that got you excited.

How were you to know
he was a vice squad detective
who would arrest you,
charge you with 'offensive behaviour'.

Given who you were,
a visiting pianist from Chile,
this sensation made the local papers.
So when you walked onto the stage
of the Sydney Town Hall
the next evening,
the audience gave you,
Claudio Arrau,
a standing ovation.

The judge agreed,
fined you five pounds
for what he considered
a completely trivial case.
The infamous were not so lucky.

Double Drowning

Violent Death At Gay Beat (Newspaper headline, 1972)

When a TV crew arrived
the body of Dr. George Duncan
had already been pulled
from the River Torrens.

At the Coronial Inquiry
three police suspects
refused to answer questions.

A former policeman
told a local paper
the police murdered Duncan
and covered it up.

At the trial
of two of these policemen,
one admitted
it was a common practice
for police to throw
homosexuals into the river.
The two were acquitted.

The companion of Duncan
thrown in at the same time
refused to give evidence.
Calls for a Royal Commission
have been ignored.

Three years after
Duncan was drowned
South Australia
became the first state
to decriminalise homosexuality.

When the TV crew arrived
the obliging police
returned the body
to the River Torrens
so the crew could film
George Duncan's recovery.

'Pray Away The Gay'

1970s

I'm a born-again Christian
so I attended an accountability session
as part of my conversion program
and had to confess to how many times
I'd masturbated since the last session,
watched gay porn, fantasised about men,
because I want to be cured,
being gay is wicked and sinful and wrong,
as the Bible has spelt out so clearly,
though I can't cope with the men
in the group moving in, heads bowed,
to pray over me. I really fancy
one of them. And I've been sent
to a counsellor who wanted to know
how often my father abused me,
and since I couldn't remember
I must have blocked it out
and now don't know who to blame
for this guilt and shame and self-loathing.
And when the counsellor invited me
back to his place for more personal
explorations I wanted to vomit,
wanted to end my life because
I can never give them what they want,
my homoerotic head on a plate.

80 'Suicides' In The 80s

better to have been straight
that night
when you went for a walk
along the cliff-top beat
when the Bondi Boys attacked
chanting *Poofter! Poofter!*
punched and kicked
using fists and boots and a hammer
breaking teeth and ribs and other bones
before they threw you
over the cliff
onto the rocks below
where we threw the other one

better to have been straight
then the police investigation
would not have ended so soon
would not have ignored evidence
would not have concluded
you died of *misadventure*
or worse   killed yourself

AIDS

a found poem based on newspaper headlines

The Man Who Gave Us Aids

AIDS kills three in Sydney

Two more suspected of having AIDS

Rare Cancer Seen In 47 Homosexuals

AIDS Risk For 647

AIDS - a grim toll builds up

The black plague of the eighties

Terror Of The Plague

Plague Brings New Havoc

My Doomed Son's Plague Agony

Grim Reaper to rise from the grave

OUTBREAK – The AIDS Trail That Lead To A Doctor's Surgery

Blood contaminated by deadly Aids

Hospital using killer blood

AIDS victim gave blood

AIDS Kills Babies

AIDS Killed Prince

Fatal homosexual disease linked to immunity

AIDS Is Germ Warfare By The US Gov't Against Gays & Blacks

Gays 'Conspired To Infect Society'

Is this the wrath of God, says Vicar.

Simple solution to A.I.D.S. is abstinence

HIV vaccine might be a step closer

AIDS epidemic 'over' in Australia, say peak bodies

Global HIV remedy faces prejudice

Newspaper headline, 2016

only half of the world's
      HIV positive population

is on anti-retroviral
      treatment

at a cost of billions
      of dollars a year

the world's most costly
      pandemic   HIV

could be wiped out
      by the preventative pill

pre-exposure prophylaxis
      or PrEP   already

slashing infection rates
      among high risk populations

so far only seven countries
      have approved its use

France is the only country
      to subsidise the drug

it's available in Australia
      for $10,000 a year

PrEP is likely to be blocked
      by discrimination

towards homosexuals
      sex workers and drug users

You Wouldn't Read About It

a found poem, 2016

homosexual revolution
a neo-Marxist agenda of cultural relativism
derivative of Queer Theory run by a Trotskyite
taking over our schools
toddlers learning about rainbow sex
creating another stolen generation
paedophiles grooming our children
men roaming free in women's bathrooms
dangerous radicals
undermining the family structure
this genderless agenda is a packaged deal
remaking society in its own radical image
silencing dissenting voices
same sex marriage is the tip of the iceberg
the slippery slope
leading to unwanted consequences
anonymous sperm donations
commercial surrogacy
inequality for children
required to miss out on a mother or father
a good old-fashioned Australian cultural war
should everyone be allowed the same aspirations?

Sorry

On 24 May, 2016 the Victorian Parliament apologised to gay men

            .

On behalf of the Parliament
the Government
and the people of Victoria
we apologise
for the laws we passed ...

In Victoria
buggery was punishable
by the death penalty
until 1949.
It was reduced
to 20 years imprisonment
then 15 years.

laws that amounted
to state-sanctioned
homophobia ...

I was crucified
by the press.

I shut down
and went overseas.

My mum was abused
by a neighbour
for having a son
like me.

We say sorry to those
we wrongly arrested ...

I wasn't allowed
to call my parents
let alone a lawyer.

I signed a statement
the police had written.

The police locked me up
and got two confessions
out of me. I was eighteen.

I was convicted
of a homosexual offence.
I was seventeen.

I was sexually abused
by my boss.
My parents reported him
to the police.
He was charged.
So was I, one count
of buggery, two counts
of gross indecency.
It was 1977.
I was fourteen.

It's about time
and it is right.
We are sorry.
Humbly, deeply
sorry.

Muscular Flirtations

The poems in 'Muscular Flirtations' focus on my personal journey down Rainbow Road, from child to adult, a parallel story to 'Inheritance'. I'm fascinated by childhood recollections. In 'The Kiss', why did an eleven year old boy store away an anti-gay reaction for later on? The older boy deals with a schoolboy crush, macho footy, first sexual experiences. The young adult struggles to accept his sexual identity, flounders through relationships. A more mature person emerges, comfortable, and happy, with the man he has become.

RW

The Kiss

I was eleven, sitting in the lounge reading,
my aunt entertaining friends
who danced around her teapot cauldron.

They speared her sponge with polite forks,
sipped milky tea, two sugars,
the pinkies raised a riot of red varnish.

They assumed I was far too young
to understand their chatter,
experts shuffling the pack of gossip,

dealing cards of sin. The one who told
a shocking story took the trick,
her voice lowered, my ears antennae.

A woman she knew had tried to kiss
another woman! Floral teacups
rattled, mouths gaped, eyebrows arched

in agitation. The words that followed
raged with indignation, stoning
the culprit to death deemed insufficient.

These were good women, attended church
each Sunday, wore hats, raised,
they thought, godly children, so this

strong revulsion made such an impact
I stored it up in case
the adult I grew into kissed a man.

Guilt Season

aged twelve   lying face down on the floor
the evening paper spread out before me
skipping the front pages   the heat   a crash
a squalid murder   it's summer   I'm staring
at the ads. for swimwear   not the women
I'm fixated on the men   black and white
sketches of beach balls   near-naked bodies
tight trunks   but no artistic suggestion
of what's underneath them   I'm forced to use
my imagination to invent the bulges
know this is wrong   fear I'll be caught
pressing my genitals into the carpet
aware of my desires   the snide taboos
unaware of how I gained this knowledge

Exclusion

The gay men of my youth
were well hidden,
referred to as homo

or poof, the name
Oscar Wilde
a snicker of hate.

A few made it
onto the silver screen,
the Tinsel Town version

of camp shop assistant
flapping his wrists
like feather dusters,

hand-on-hip mincing,
his few lines a susurrus
of the sibilant S,

a role model I was keen
to avoid. Yet I drooled
over the more macho

Gary Cooper, Rock Hudson,
Montgomery Clift, butch
names for butch personas,

the Hollywood lie.
Pummelled from youth
to adult, I too tried to hide,

dressed to kill, a sparkling
wit to cover the sorrow,
postures that gave me away.

The one I managed to kill
was my true self.
He took his revenge.

Je Suis/Nous Sommes

they know you're not one of them
but can't say why   you're here
to make up the numbers   fill

the empty desk at the back
of the room where no other boy
will join you   where your arm

never gives the Nazi salute
to answer a question   and since
you haven't learnt the verbs set

for homework   the French teacher
orders you to stand up straight
hold out your trembling hand

it pulls back as he strikes the air
with his steel ruler   so you're
hit across the knuckles twice

the pain not as bad as this
isolation   you will learn
how to negotiate friendship

watching other boys   their
banter   their dalliances
their sudden bursts of fists

and making-up   what it takes
to establish your own identity
je suis/tu es/il est   what

it takes to avoid difference
nous sommes/vous etes/ils sont
the verbs needed for conjugation

Idolatry

there was an older boy at school
I idolised   and kept it secret

not for his looks   he was no
Rock Hudson   had gaunt

features   skin pulled tight
over tidy bones   wisps of hair

but he was a fast runner
the athlete we cheered the most

on sports days   a bony chest
lifting to receive the medals

I fantasised about joining him
on the track   he'd teach me

how to spurt out from the blocks
time my dash to the finish line

pat my shoulder in the showers
the seal of a slight smile enough

to encourage me   but it wasn't
sport that drew me to him

he was much admired   but
like me   spent his time alone

on the oval training   or sitting
on his own at lunchtime staring

at other boys   as if ...   I felt
the ache of an enigmatic empathy

the invisible thread that linked us
that broke when he left school

some years ago I read that he
had died   AIDS   judging

by his youth   the guarded
wording   I see him sprinting

through the stars   a flash of light
too fast for death to catch

Footy

every Saturday morning   on the school oval
I was made to play   had no ability
but could run fast   used this skill
to avoid the pack   the scrum   the violent
push and thump and yell   alpha males
manhandling their way to warriors
leaders   lovers   mounting   in control
I kept my distance   too afraid
I'd be knocked over   injured   maimed
if   by accident   a football landed
in my arms   I'd kick it away
in any direction except towards team mates
or our goals   before some thug
tackled me   brought me down   when
it was all over   whether we won or lost
I didn't care   I was too embarrassed
to expose my puny body in the showers
all those big boys   their wet soapy flesh
covered in hairs   muscular voices   those
hungry jokes about girls   I feigned indifference
glimpsed their manhood when they changed
clothed my muddy body   hurried home
aroused   uncomfortable   ashamed

1950s Boys

waves of summer heat
couldn't wash away the stains

of how we loved   lying
face down on the lawn

where   later that evening
my aunt would practice croquet

smacking the balls so hard
I thought she'd seen us

you behind me   your hand
snaking up my leg and under

my shorts   in search of a snake
finding it   I lay hypnotised

as if unmoved   then the hours
to kill before bed time   before

darkness concealed our devilry
sitting in the caravan

you slept in   rock music
on your transistor   crickets

crooning   a croquet ball
across the road hitting a hoop

we sat apart   too bashful
to go further   to reach out

and touch identity   youth
the dagger unsheathed between us

1960s Men

you enter the rain
        and arrive at his flat

wet through   you don't know
        how to love a man

yet   conditioning has created
        too much ambivalence

he makes you strip off
        dries your clothes

in front of the heater
        the gas splutters and pops

he's beside you on the couch
        shoes and socks off

his stretched-out feet
        playing with yours

first steps towards oblivion
        his gentle touch

breaks your kneecap
        you shiver   light closes in

as he moves nearer
        a hand reaches out

you jump into damp clothes
        that stick to your skin

and rush from the room
        he stands at the door

waving his warmed penis
        and still you run

When We Were Alive

1

I remember the evenings, and the sky
filled with stars stretched over a wide street,

and wind stripping the plane trees
of their paper bag leaves, and you arriving

home late, and wedging your body
next to mine, and the friction of flesh

and hands and nakedness provoking
the excitement of a forbidden game,

and I remember the gasping pleasure
in your eyes, when the earth flashed

faster on its axis, and as the wind stilled
we sheltered in each other's arms

wondering whether this was about love
or sex or loneliness or simply pain,

and I remember the sounds of the night
curling up in the dark corners of the room.

A tattoo inked into the skin of memory.
A comet splashing into a sea of loss.

2

I remember the mornings, and a radiator
bar of sunlight sharp under the blind,

heat clogging up the bedroom, smothering
the air, and furniture emerging from blurred

shadows, returning us to the reality
of the ordinary world after last night's joy,

and you curled up tight behind me,
our legs tangled, an arm over my shoulder

as you whispered his name, and I remember
how sex tasted like chalk in the mouth,

dry and bitter, an emptiness longing
could not assuage, and when a shrill

ambulance siren blasted the street outside,
you woke and stretched and angled

your arms over your head, and I remember
I leant in close, doubting, to smell love.

A wanton cupid armed with golden desires.
A poisoned arrow dipped in jealousy.

The 7 Basic Plots

according to Christopher Booker

1. Overcoming the Monster

As a young man I lived
in someone else's country, too afraid
to give my difference a name.
On the outside, looking in
on happiness. When I embraced
my incubus I embraced myself.

2. Rags to Riches

Please Sir, I'd like some more.
Like Oliver I was begging,
lurched from famine to famine
until I met him, a dish
too rich for someone as inexperienced
as me. I gobbled him up.

3. The Quest

Having tasted my first quarry
I set off to unearth more.
Slayed them, betrayed them,
lost my way and lost count,
the Holy Grail of the perfect match
dissolving in the desert.

4. Comedy

Went on our first date overdressed,
looking like a rainbow lorikeet.
Dribbled down my shirt.
Gabbled. Drank too much.
Fell asleep before he could lay a hand
on me. He left his business card.

5. Tragedy

When I came out to my family
my mother said, *I'll always love you.*
And we won't talk about it
ever again. It felt as if
she'd put a hand on my face,
crumpled it like a piece of paper.

6. Rebirth

I'd been drifting until I met you,
your love the lifejacket
that keeps me bobbing
over the waves. A fellowship
that has remade me, selfish
to selfless, chaos to calm.

7. Voyage and Return

Ours is a long journey, shaping
our history in slow motion.
Now that it's speeded up, time
changing sides, trapped by the pain
of angry bones, we've reached a beginning,
start again in a new world.

Leaving Home, And Returning

1

you act like a ship hooting
as it sails for The Heads

the city that's left behind
a gutter of deep secrets
failed romance   your identity

in crisis   your family
picks up the padlock and chains

to save for next time   lines up
for the ambivalent waving
your smile embraces the widening

gap between ship and pier
the rough seas of the unknown

you unpack tomorrow
in your cabin   give the steward
a wink   a generous tip

2

you feel like a plane shuddering
as it comes in to land
the city below a life

of faltering lights   dirty stories
somewhere a dog baying

home a quixotic museum
of plaster cast busts
the padlocked family

who speak in riddles
clutch at old photos

you attack a wall
with a sledgehammer
step through the rubble

someone waits for you
on the other side   staring

Vandalism

... *the last thing to go is ... the signature, the home of personhood*
Oliver Sacks

mother reacted with an embrace
said she would always love you
don't ever mention it again

the afternoon an envelope
licked and sealed   posted
to an unknown destination

your body reduced to a shadow
covered in wounds   identity
a story deprived of words

grandmother didn't embrace you
stood back from the disease
offered to pay for your treatment

the room a surgery   emotions
disinfected   blunt instruments
meticulous on a steel tray

your shadow reduced to a knife
you carved your initials
into a tree   they have survived

Gay Bar

a shadowy pool
teems with eyes
swimming over you

hungry for flesh
to assuage
years of hostility

and regret
with at least
one piranha

who'll move in
and strip you
to the bone

the barman
a tease away
from fantasy's touch

a cocktail of tattooed
smiles, muscular
flirtations

alcohol a means
to transcend
sweating uncertainties

you drink enough
to numb
the reservations

vanish into
the shoal of night
with somebody

wake in the morning
with a terror
stranger than sex

Pattern

all the men you have hooked up with
in bars or at parties or behind
a bookshop shelf   eyes that lifted
from pages into possibilities   into
beds   where hands smoothed out
the creases of alone   lips healed
the wounds of words   flesh stretched
over exhausted flesh   only to wake
in the musty swamp of morning
embarrassed by the night's reckless risks
men you permitted to take possession
to presume another time   raising hopes
of long term not having to look further
when you dumped them
was this payback for the first man
Mr Dark Haired Dark Eyed Handsome
who seduced you   entered you so hard
the pain screamed   the one who left you
waiting for his summons   then left you
and all the men after were brief chapters
in your Book Of Dark Haired Men
you earmarked and beguiled and abandoned

Manners

when you look back you're astonished
by your hypocrisy   those two faces
the one that hid from your mother
what you had done the night before
with that man   down on your knees
or spread across his bed   his hands
his greed   his ardent savagery
mother thought she had taught you
how to behave   her *sit up straight*
not meant to be in that position
gasps of pain   of pleasure   not part
of her elocution lessons   sexual
exhaustion not quite the elegant
sufficiency she had in mind   though
she would have been impressed
with your good manners   *please*
to begin with   *thank you* at the end

Hot and Cold

I'm sure my grandparents
never had sex in their shower

I did   grandfather underground
grandmother on the widow's tour

of South East Asia   which meant
I had the house to myself

I invited him over   naked
we slipped over the wet tiles

hot water and steam and soap
working up a playful lather

no need for words   just hands
exploring our liquid bodies

afterwards we rolled about
in the ancient double bed

its lumpy mattress
that sagged in the middle

not needing an excuse
to be bundled together

later grandmother returned
gave me a cheap tourist trinket

I kept my more expensive
souvenirs to myself

the bruise on my neck   a groin
that itched   abandonment

The Hours Alone

1

Keenness for an experience I've never had
     brings me to this encounter on the beach.

I'm stretched beside the dark determined man
     who I caught watching when I danced,

a look that signalled his intent, those eyes
     etched into my body's sinuous steps.

The sun setting alight expectations, wind
     scribbling a salty omen on my skin.

He produces oil, rubs my burning shoulders,
     massages a message into my back.

Little is said, words struggle then sink
     under the waves two strangers make.

After a swim, towelling off further delays,
     we leave together, heading for his flat.

I look back, see that I have left behind
     the imprint of my loneliness on the sand.

2

We are stopped at a red light,
my hand on his knee
the ache of reassurance.

I want to see him
more often. I can't say it
aloud, I'll frighten him off.

Outside the night
spits and kicks.

He clings to the steering
braced for take-off.
Talks about work
and other diversions,
anything but us. And me?
I'm his willing prisoner
in the cell of desire.

Rain hits the windscreen
like dollops of ink.

He revs my engine,
slips me into gear.

3

He's smoking a post-coital
cigarette, my head soft
on his shoulder, fingers

entwining the black hairs
on his chest. I cannot ask
why we are here in this motel,

asking well might undermine
what this feels like: used.
Forcing me to face my complicity,

forcing me to face the hours alone,
stretched like fencing wire,
waiting for a call to his side.

He's watching the smoke drift
to the ceiling. It will still be there
trapped until I leave.

Aftershave

you left me that day   after I dragged you
in out of the sun   its heat splitting
heads open   tore at the brevity
of your clothes   fondled you into arousal
my tongue wet in your ear
and down your neck   the musky smell
of your aftershave all the aphrodisiac
I needed   the fierce weight of you
on the disfigured bed   taking control
your teeth a punishment   nipping
reproaches into my flesh   the sun
a knife through the window that severed
the cord   your eyes hovered near mine
slipped off me as the door closed

Tradie

he arrives at the back door
wearing the uniform   T shirt
under flannel   grubby shorts

takes his boots off   his one
concession to our tidy home
before he deconstructs it

my description of the job
elicits mumbles   his eyes
like a tape measuring me up

his trade is noise   hammering
planning   the radio in his ute
rocks the neighbourhood

and tools   a motley collection
of the sharp   blunt   forensic
that legitimise his trade

I keep a reverent distance
but have to watch   muscles
that stretch the tattoos   sweat

slicking carcinogenic skin
thick and stubborn fingers
that grapple and hold and tug

manhandling my fantasies
until he squats   exposes
the down side of temptation

I clean up the rubble
after he skyrockets off
in a scream of gravel

grateful for the repairs
that might last   the eye
candy   celestial silence

Priest

You take the steps down to our front door
one at a time, as if your knees
buckle under the weight of prayer.

The small bag you carry
for an overnight stay, clinks.
It doesn't sound like pyjamas,

a change of underwear, a stringent
volume on the lives of the saints
you've struggled, for years, to emulate.

You greet both of us with a hug,
cling on much longer than we wanted,
a candle lit for an urgent need.

In the kitchen you open the bag,
produce two bottles of wine,
a bottle of whisky. Nothing else.

This is an act of generosity.
Or it measures the religious life,
the toll it's taken on your sexuality.

You begin our meal with a prayer,
celebrate friendship, proud, and envious,
of us, a pair of beads on your rosary.

We are reduced to a congregation.
Your sermon, eased with the blood
of Christ, is a litany of anniversaries:

the day you first met my partner
in a church. The year that he left
the seminary. And after ordination,

the stations of your cross, a thorny journey
through promotions to smaller, and smaller
parishes, a snide excommunication.

You have devoted your life to Jesus,
now you admit you wish his name
had been Damian or Angelo or Ben.

We listen in silence to this disclosure,
not surprised, but not comfortable
in this confessional, our roles reversed.

No amount of Hail Marys, no blessings,
no forgiveness of sins, can compensate
for the years of sacrifice, and denial.

You leave the next morning, each step
a retreat back to seclusion, each
intake of breath a whisper withdrawn.

Portrait Of A Near-naked Man

after Marcus Wills: The Ersatz *(Ballarat Art Gallery)*

You cannot know his past,
where he comes from,
why he's here. His head

bent down, eyes hard to see
and focused on the floor.
Is he ashamed of his near

nakedness? Is this humility
or an unwillingness
to engage in your stare?

Light blushed along his neck,
surges of passion
subdued on his chest,

a fist curled with craving.
You are tempted to reach out,
touch the trembling lustre

of his flesh, stubbled hair,
provocative bulges
that stretch the thin briefs.

If he raised his head
and looked straight at you,
the energy of paint

bursting through his skin,
you'd be unmasked, discovered.
You'd be somebody else.

OCD, A Survivor's Manual

My breakfast routine, preparing the tea,
           twin bowls of muesli, the cutlery
laid down with regimental reverence,

is my attempt to drive the world's car
           that's out of control, my foot
on the brake as it races faster.

Light through the kitchen window
           offers a benign calm, a diversion
that sharpens autumn's rusted colours.

A blue wren skitters through leaves
           the wind has shuffled up under
the elms, a messenger of vitality.

My partner appears in black pyjamas.
           Sleep has once again dodged him,
driven off by aggressive hits of pain.

I watch his body as it lurches,
           the top half bent forward, a face
that fights to muster a smile.

I can't help but think about
           how he used to be, fit and fast
and healthy, an unstoppable spirit,

until the twin blades of life's
           cruel weapons, age and illness,
diminished his independence.

He sits down, winces. I pass him
           the milk, pour his cup of tea,
arrange the paper for him to read.

Outside a chaotic wind blusters
           through the trees. Dark clouds cluster
at the sky's edge, ready to take over.

I line up the plates and cutlery
            on the sink in their usual order.
At least I can make them clean.

This is my racing car helmet:
            routine, acceptance, togetherness
that fortify me for the crash.

the stare that transfixes us

the stare that transfixes us
across an indifferent room
launches our poem in silence

you smile a simile
that invites interpretation
lures me into closer contact

you whisper in my ear
lyrical oblations
to the god of seduction

I'm won over   in bed
hands caress flesh   read
the lucid Braille of our bodies

those signals we translate
into the aroused words
of our impassioned verse

asleep in my arms

asleep in my arms
he breathes
into a snuffled dream
his head a cushion
for my chin
as I lean in
smell his sweaty secrets

cuddling him
won't be enough
to save us
from this delirious world
its cankerous delusions
but when he stirs
clings tighter
our breaths eased
into breathless singularity
this intimate moment
puts the apocalypse on hold

Naked Truth

you know all about difference
when very young   which is when
they teach you to hate yourself
words unravel from their tongues
the tips of the fangs poisoned
define why you are on the outside
looking in   will never belong
will never be accepted or loved
unless you change   unless
you become one of them
or remove yourself altogether
many will conform   create a carapace
that might fool some people
but deep inside stands
the blazing glory of who you really are
and this mighty hurricane of truth
will sweep all the debris away
and leave you standing naked
scarred   imperfect   a column
of light   an infinite illumination

Astronauts

I doubt if I will find another one
like you   time and constant wear
allow me to ease into the comfort
of your slippered self   forgiveness smiles
from Tartar eyes   yet you are harried
by afflictions   and age has left your skull
bald   there's a pattern not unlike
the blemish on the moon   we two
have flown there   took our own
giant step for mankind   the view
from the other side soothed us
yet we were happier when the world
welcomed us home   if I'm kept awake
at night it's because you are singing
in your sleep   a lunar language
impossible to decipher   it leaves me time
to think about the choice I made
to love you   I too will sing
until obscured by the next lunar eclipse

Selected Poems

The Match Of The Hunter – 1998

My Life As A Sheep Dog – 2009

Man In A Glass Suit – 2011

An Elegant Sufficiency – 2015

Caught Jesting – 2018

from *The Match Of The Hunter*

1998

Gift From Prometheus

We planted trees
as risky as gelignite
around our inflammable homes
and watched them explode.

Wind plays host
to this plague,
pumping its veins uphill
from the match of the hunter.

Now brown leaves
fall like confetti
from the aching ruins
and blacken our memory.

We married this
binary god of fire,
knowing his retribution
could burn more than our fingers.

Yet we must live
chained to these hills
and fathom our equipoise
by seeing, not by love.

A Shot In The Dark

Yes I'm clairvoyant, I can
see your pain, can see
the needled anguish
in your face, can hear
the jagged glass that cut

the child, the terrors
in your mind-erasing past.
Can scream the journey
trickling through your blood,
the thumping of desire

to crucify, to nail upon
the cross the one that bent
and touched and made you cry.
Guilt, the first injection,
the kick into the guts that

spills your thirst, and followed
by remorse and worthlessness
and nowhere else to go,
rebounding in some harsh
archaic voice that only I

can silence and decode.
The youth in you,
the running far away,
your smile embedded in
the passing trade.

Dissolve in me. Let me lick
your arms, thread my fingers
through your bletted veins.
I'm doting seamstress treadling
through your wares. I need.

On Choosing Death

We must love one another or die. (W. H. Auden).

Loving one another
is almost impossible,

like shedding tears
underwater
or dancing a tango
on ice.

To love one another
is to smile at hate,
to take envy
by the hand
and lead it savagely
into forgiveness.

To love one another
is to find the words
and hurl them
like knives
at the moon,
the sky's turbulent
cycle of lust.

Easier to die
and leave behind
a crepuscular shell
unsullied by risk
or desire.

Shells this empty though
make brittle monuments.

Nothing

Nothing comes to us
stamped 'yours forever'
but why change forests

into something else?
Trunks of ivy, aluminium
plants, a branch of feral

cat and bark of fox.
What was wrong with
light that laces tree ferns,

a moss-ribbed creek that
sweeps the sentient gum,
a liquid maze of leaves,

a bird that mocks
and mimics our decay?
A forest of tree souls

rarely smells of rain,
it squints into the sun
and casts no shadow.

from *My Life As A Sheep Dog*

2009

My Life As A Sheep Dog

I learnt to swear in my uncle's paddocks,
rounding up the sheep with the black
sheep dog he had named Nigger.
Go round Nigger, go round ya fuckin' idiot.
Nigger sank to the ground and waited.
Stay Nigger stay ya fuckin' bastard,
as Nigger shot into the pack
and nipped a sheep on its back leg.
The sheep headed in every direction
except the gate my uncle had opened.
You go and round them up Robbie,
Nigger's fuckin' useless. I ran like a soldier
bolting the trenches at Gallipoli,
sprinting round the flock with Nigger
at my side obeying my every oath.
The sheep responded and trotted through the gate
as meekly as lambs. Uncle then drove his ute
down the centre of the road, waving aside
other drivers, the sheep followed in a tight pack,
Nigger and me bringing up the rear.

At the abattoirs sheep went into bleating panic.
Men in bloodied white aprons slit their throats
over metal grills, hung them from rails
by the feet and ripped wool and skin down
to their swinging heads then knifed stomachs open,
entrails slipping onto the floor like a birth,
the offal tossed into piles, or tossed at me.
The stench, the steam, the hot water hoses,
the swearing that was intended to render
a brutal occupation a touch more bearable
were easily absorbed into my child's mind.

When I returned to my home in the suburbs
and said to my sister, *It's your turn*
to wash the fuckin' dishes, I soon learnt
the difference between country and city.

Pier

In the summer of childhood
I raced along the pier,
leaping over the gaps
between splintered planks,
afraid the sea would slip through
like a wet tongue
and swallow me.

Passed the fisherman
hunched over his line,
a Rodin statue reeling in
memories of the catch.
Felt the spray dousing
my face in brine,
the sun watering my eyes.

At the end of the pier
I gripped the rail
and watched the waves,
scared I'd be swept overboard,
my skin gouged by barnacles
that armoured the pylons.

My gaze trapped
by the horizon
where sea and sky
met in a line so thin
there was no chance
I could squeeze through
and shed my childhood.

Footprints In The Ashes

In the club rooms at the local sports oval,
after evacuation, we were offered drinks
and food. One man turned on the TV
so we could watch our houses burning down
on the evening news. Clenched around tables,
we licked our fears with sandpaper tongues.
A social worker in an evening dress
asked my neighbour why she was there.
Because there's a fire, she said, and choked.

The next day we stood facing the ruins,
a wall of stillness where the front gate
had been, where so many have stood before,
arms interlocked, fingers dug into flesh.

Our green landscape had melted
from the canvas, replaced by a sketch
in black and grey. Contorted shapes.
Ashes. Winded silence. A charred stench
that burnt a hole in our memories forever.

Warped roofing iron lay strewn about
as if the vanishing house had collapsed
underground into a burial mound,
the chimney left standing like a stalagmite.
The house not only a loss of timber,
paper, clay, but a routine
we would spend years chasing.

Where the lounge room wall
had harboured our shelves of books,
layers of pages in white ash
made ghostly reading, the words
waiting to be effaced by touch
or rain or the cruelty of wind.

The madness of loss drove us to trawl
the ruins for mementos. Pottery emerged
all the better for a second firing,
except for bubbles of glass
welded to the sides like fattened tears
streaking a blistered face.
Then shudders of rain turned ash
into mud, flattened the breath out of smoke.
Trees scattered their leaves like confetti.
Relief was marred by a tribal scream:
Why now? No one asked us about the cat.

Three days later we collected unmarked
garden furniture before looters struck.
The clothesline had already vanished.

A crude sign on the main road announced:
'Looters Will Be Shot'. The cat turned up.
Unscathed. Wisdom that comes
from knowing about wombat holes.
I had never seen my family cry like that.

Mountain Ash

too many questions
are wrapped around
the base of a tree
distracting me each
time I drive through
this part of the forest
along with flowers
impossibly blooming
from a eucalypt
a mountain ash that
unlike abrupt mortals
remains impervious
to the rings of years

until this moment

until this placing
of flowers and a square
of white cardboard
with the crucified
names of two brothers
who assumed youth
ensured they would
live the length of
a mountain ash

only the cockatoos
screeching overhead
like a car's tyres
suggest an answer

Vicious Circle

I lift the bird
from the sludge
with black gloves,
plunge it into
detergent then
sponge and rinse,
sponge and rinse,
stroking through
the warp and weft
of its wings,
its underbelly
until the colours
begin to emerge.

The bird remains
inert, as if fully
cognisant of
my ministrations,
as if discerning,
with its round eyes,
head half-cocked,
the difference between
a saviour's baptism
and the sackcloth
and ashes of our sins.

After nurturing
the bird is released
back into water
just in time for
the loading of guns.

Bone Collector

a soldier once
his next weapon
became the metal
detector he shouldered
like a gun

mined the bones
of dead comrades
their bodies left to rot
where they fell
on the Kokoda Track

his platoon's
only survivor
he emerged from
the jungle scarred
and wasted away

years later
the promise he made
was more important
than the wife and children
he left behind

the bones
returned to families
still grieving for
the proud sons
of the fatherland

now a temple bell
summons an old
man to prayer
his tears dried
in the red sun

Silent Partner

She waits by the shoreline
and numbers the waves

scudding onto the sand
an oyster-shell sky overhead

and the smell of rain
coalescent with brine

hoping this one day
he will spend with her.

She devotes her weeks
to office efficiency

redefines the mantra
that's beyond duty

in her determination
to erase the silence

and avoids weekends
by driving into the country

its dry hills and plains
defoliated by drought.

He will not come today
prefers to remain hidden

in his coastal bunker
or has gone fishing

mesmerised by the spin
of the reel, the waves

clipping the air, the zig
zag dash of the line

the fish he'll unhook
and give back to the sea

incapable of kill
and gut and scale

the blood too real
the breath too easily

taken in the jungles
of Vietnam where

to return a captive
alive was not an option.

To No Avail

Loneliness is not being alone, it's loving others to no avail. (Mario Stefani).

The glass pinning your note down
on the kitchen table is a knife
thrust through the paper-thin layer
of my trust, the words like crackling
static on a faulty line
and all I can decipher
is the horror story
about finding someone else.
I search for signs
that you were here, your smell
tangled in the sheets, a hair
wired to a bathroom towel,
you handprint I imagine
on a half-empty mug of tea,
all arranged in the shrine
I've created in my mind
where I pour libations and pray
your new lover will vaporise
and you'll rush back to me.
The screen has gone blank,
the phone is dead and something
deep inside me rolls over
and hides in an empty corner
keening like a dog.

The Week After

I expect you to return
at any moment,
your presence reduced
to stray objects
that begin to decompose.

I can still hear your car
slide into the garage
and shut down, the hand
brake a cracked knuckle
jerked into finality.

Then your steps on the path
crushing leaves that seep
from a fractured sky.

My prepared meal frozen
in time, your favourite
marinated lamb with Greek
salad, a glass of wine
refilling my failure
to absolve your absence.

I ignore the cards that line up
on the mantelpiece
like bits of shrapnel, the words
inside a crude distillation
of the truth I thought
we were still living.

My hand whipping a curtain
aside, my wet-leaved eyes
encompassing the empty path
you refuse to take, the one
I must travel to escape the words
that refuse to remain silent.

Waltzing The Weasel

a tribute to Don Watson

All right listen up stakeholders,
I want to get down to our
core business straight away.
Basically I've called this meeting
to gather feedback
for a PowerPoint Presentation
that will inform our thinking
at the post middle-management level
and to engage deeply
with the concepts that underpin
the possible initiatives
that might enhance
our competitive advantage
and ensure we achieve
world's best practice.
For realistically speaking
the fact of the matter is
it's the outcomes-based clients
who are our strategy focus
and this can only be achieved
at the end of the day
by sound knowledge management
and information processing
and by avoiding
any aggressive indifference
or negatively impacted adjustments.
Or perhaps put another way
the bottom line is
we need to engage
in exciting the industry
by expanding the package
of our key deliverables
being particularly the case
given our structural
adjustment authority
and our going forwards
to ensure future-proofing.

Any questions?

You Are Invited

At the art exhibition nobody looked
at the art, despite the title:
'The Edge Of The Other Side',
the artist a post post-modernist
of the post-tonal realist school.
Instead they elbowed others aside
to grab a glass of wine, raked
claws through bowls of crisps,
platters of finger food, eyed the room
for acquaintances, made their bee lines
and pounced, clucking and strutting
in their feathery finery.

A Senior Lecturer in the Visual Arts
from a university nobody had heard of
delivered an address to launch the show,
describing the works as:
light and shadow transmogrified
into illusion that defied logic and often
made unceasing demands on the unsaid,
strung together with 'far be it for me'
and 'be that as it may'
and ending 'without further ado'.

One lonely red dot highlighted,
in a dark corner, the single painting sold,
the over-excited purchaser nailing
the artist to the wall to share
her investment expertise and the profit
she'd make when he moved to God's Gallery.

Slow Poem

just relax   settle back   in   a comfortable

    armchair   put on   your favourite

slow   tempo   music   Gorecki's Symphony

    Of Sorrowful Songs   perhaps   and take

    several

    deep

    breaths

because   this poem   is going to   take

    quite   a long time   to   digest

try a   small bite   first   roll it   around

    in   your   mouth   chew

    a few   words   taste the similes   lick

the alliteration   like rosemary   and

    honey   and a trickle   of   lemon

    a leg of lamb   poem   on this   old

    fashioned   praise the Lord   and

pass the verses   kind of   Sunday

Donkey Serenade

When I was five
my kinder held a concert
at the end of the year
and I thought this
was the most exciting event
in the entire world.
The highlight was a dance
to 'The Donkey Serenade'.
The plum role was the donkey,
you got to wear a papier mache
donkey's head. I begged,
pleaded, cried, cajoled
and was given the part.
At the dress rehearsal
I was so carried away wearing
the mask for the first time
I stuck my bottom out
and pretended to fart.
I lost the role. I begged,
pleaded, cried, so, to shut
me up, I was allowed to appear
on stage alone and recite
a poem my mother
had taught me called 'Mud Pies'
I've never forgotten the faces
of those adoring mothers.
I decided then and there
that it was much better
to recite poetry solo on stage
than to be some farty old
donkey in a crowd scene.

from *Man In A Glass Suit*

2011

Centres Of Silence

what we've confiscated
from recent arrivals
will hardly make
any of us wealthy

cheap watches
slipping over wrists
won't be needed here

diaries
covering up the tracks
of bloodshed
and betrayal

photographs
from truncated pasts
they're lucky
to have escaped

paper
language
torn addresses

and shoelaces

we can't afford
martyrs
or escapees

their clothes
stricken with memories
we had to burn

the new uniforms
turning shoulders
into coat hangers

the barber
shaving heads
with a conviction
that belies his fear
of trauma
and mutilation
their names
rendered legal
by numbers so much
easier to pronounce
a weapon against

old enmities
smuggled inside
via bodily cavities

their first meal
a scratching of forks
over hardened plates

dreams gassed
into smoke and ashes

outside in the yard
the flies of sunlight
knuckled into
the edges of eyes
staring beyond
the barbed wire
desert of freedom

Love Letter

What he sees from the window
holds him transfixed,
his body iced up enough
to suggest rigor mortis,

    unable to move since
    he still has the letter
    glued to his hand
    (an excuse, of sorts,
    for not rushing outside)
    in a room that threatens
    a total eclipse,
    as if someone
    has switched daylight off,

the snake tossed into the air
like a comma of rope,
the dog a mirage of fur
and teeth and snapping jaws.

    In the seconds it takes
    to reread the sentence,
    the one that renders
    all other sentences invisible,
    the words inside the sentence
    rearing up, fangs bared
    to deliver their venom,

the snake has vanished, leaving
the dog left stretched on the lawn,
its legs twitching in the last
running thrusts of its death.

Hell's Ancients

A fistful of bikies
knuckle into town,
a procession
of helmeted beetles
hunched over handlebars,
black leather armour
covered in words
that backfire with menace,
conjuring up visions
of thug and brute and bash
and chains and punch,
of fight and brawl
and drugs and guns and death.

Outside a coffee shop
they sit in the sun
and sip their lattes,
their heads bald
or ringed with grey fluff,
salt-and-pepper beards,
sagging tats
and bloated paunches,
and fire salvos at each other:
how's your veggie patch
going Keith,
anyone got any blockout,
how about sharing
that lemon tart? One
is on his mobile to his wife:
hope ya coping
with the grandkids Love,
I'll be back in an hour.
And soon they crawl home.

The Perfect Host

When Macbeth came to dinner
I was out of haggis
so I started with a soup.

I was pleased to see
he washed his hands first.

Hope you like mutton broth,
I said, to break the ice.
As long as it's not fillet
of a fenny snake, newt's eyes,
toe of frog or owlet's wing,
I've had a belly full of that,
he snapped. He was not
in a happy frame of mind.

He ate with little appetite
but drank a lot.

I tried to cheer him up.
For the main course
you could have either
nose of Turk, Tartar's lips
or finger of a birth-strangled,
I quipped. He thumped
the table with his fist.
Accursed be the tongue
that tells me so.
If thou speak'st true
upon the next tree
shalt thou hang alive.

It was but a jest Sire, I said,
and served the bangers and mash.

How's the little wife getting on?
I asked, to lighten the mood.
Enjoying the perks of high office?

She's not herself. Thick caring
fancies keep her from her rest.
The doctor's useless, says
she must minister to herself.
Who'd pay for that advice?
Oh if only we'd had children.

He was playing with his food
by now. I took his plate away
and poured more wine.

Perhaps a holiday? I suggested.

I thought of taking her camping
at Birnam Wood
but some bastard's
cut all the trees down.

What about England?

Full of my enemies,
Malcolm, Macduff, Banquo.

Isn't Banquo... dead my Lord?

Him too? Gone, all gone.
He looked miserable.
In desperation I suggested
we get out the Ouija board,
see if we could get a laugh
by contacting Macduff's mother
and asking her about childbirth.
Lay on, he cried, rallying to,
and dammed be him
that first cries: Board, enough!

from *An Elegant Sufficiency*

2015

Speaking up for those men

after Arundhathi Subramaniam

I want to speak up
for those men
with comb overs
stretching long hairs
like guitar strings

who hitch their trousers
up under their armpits

who wear socks with sandals
in case they get wet feet

whose love life
was swallowed by a sink-hole

who spent
their entire working life
in a denture clinic

who have a different denture
for each day of the week

none of them fit properly

whose social life
is focused
on a poker machine

who never
did anyone any harm

who still believe
they'll meet the right woman

these men with comb overs
I want to speak up for them.

When Love Came

I thought I'd recognise
love when it came
given its reputation
good to look at
charming   urbane
holding me close
in an embrace
of honeyed flame
fanning my wild
spirits   teaching me
passion's fiery
kisses   flesh
melted into flesh
the same drum
beating to one refrain

how little I knew
of life's entrapments
not knowing love came
unexpected   plain

Bottled Love

I sent you a message in a bottle,
asking you to spend the rest of your life
with me. Walked to the end of a pier
and tossed the bottle into the sea.
Dwarfed by the surge of waves
its axis tilted towards the tide of hope.
When it washes up on your beach,
barnacled, salted, seaweed glazed,
I want you to untangle its contents,
read the signs. Read more than the words
I have crafted with the ache of desire.
Read into those watermarks, here is a love
that will endure the upheaval of ocean,
the crab-like crawl of setting time.

Forgotten Love

The letter fell from the book
I was culling,
Laclos' *Dangerous Liaisons*
as it happens.
Not that I want to read
too much into that.

The writing had paled
into significance, his fanciful
loops circling all manner
of disturbances.

Reading it again
after so many years
of partnered solitude,
I relived the sexual frisson,
the urgency, the retreat.

I want to be with you,
he wrote. *I walk
along our beach where waves
ripple the pages of our love.*
I can still picture his long
strides, fingers snapping
to curb the dog's freedom,
the fierce, hurried charm
of his embrace.

I'll love you forever ...
which gave eternity
a briefer definition. *But
I can't leave her just yet.*
Which brought the point
of his sword to my throat.

Is he still with her, shrouding
his true self in the tomb
of marriage? Still stalking
men in the alley of delusion?

My knuckles whitened.
I crumpled the letter
in my fist. I thought
I was beyond being dragged
into its mythology.
What must remain hidden,
what must be understood.
Its malign betrayals.

Love Sonnet

After a life of amorous loving
our passion has been transformed.
Gone are youth's meteorites
hurtling through heavens, slamming
into earth, sending up clouds
of lust and doubt. Now we orbit
the same moon, lapped in a blue
shimmer, becalmed by time.
The questions answered, the words
primed to offer forgiveness.
Love has become a merging
of two harmonic tides,
your tears still in my eyes,
my smile gentle on your lips.

Sea Trinity

for Jill and John Sutton

My back's dysfunctional after
a fractured sleep
on my friends' futon,
they're heavily into
the transcendental
discomfort of Zen
and bouts of psychodrama
to disentangle the meaning
of fallen fruit.

Yet I manage our walk
along the shore,
the view so rhapsodic
my pain is laundered.

It's the ocean
hypnotically teasing,
elbowed into the coast,
its fleshy waves
massaging the sand's vertebrae.

I'm transfixed by a heron
a pen-stroke away
from a Japanese print,
its toothpick legs slicing
rice paper shallows,
head stilled as an arrow
to target a fish.

The three of us
a sea trinity
after a tidal break,
the beach a whiteboard
where our footprints
are swiftly erased
despite our brittle attempts
to leave a mark,
the wind consuming
our past's disquietude.

Horses

We heard them first,
hoofs beating the road
like a drum, forcing
the charge louder, closer.

When they arrived outside,
singular black horses
only one was white,
they waited in silence,
stamping their sweat
into the ground,
skin flinching as if
electrical currents
passed through them,
mnemonic globular eyes
staring at sorrow.

Echoes of ancestors
who had dragged ploughs,
gone blind in the pits,
buckled into the mud
to the whisper of bombs,
fell at the jump
and had to be shot.

And their ears twitched
anticipating more terrors,
a virus on the wing,
poisonous orange clouds,
the ocean rising.

When they moved on
we sensed they had
harnessed the world
and pulled it behind them,
out of the chaos,
out of the mud,
and we were drawn
into the same breathing.

Splash

after David Hockney's painting 'A Bigger Splash'

His Californian boy
has been engulfed,
completely vanished,
victim of his
insatiable need to blend
flesh with water.

The diving board
no longer pulsating,
foot-print free.

All that is left
is the split second,
the white patch
smudging
an ice-cube pool.

The chair dwarfed
by the flat-roofed house
and two palm trees
cutting parallel tracks
across the sky.

The chair
where the diver
plotted his escape,
rested his smooth skin,
taut belly,
trembling limbs.

The Portrait Of Oscar Wilde

There are several ways to commit
suicide. One infallible method
is to be infatuated

with a beautiful young man
hell-bent on patricide.
It helps to have an ego

the size of a long-running play,
bathing each night
in that hip-bath of milk, applause.

To believe your wit
can unravel a judge,
publicly shame a pugilist

with a spelling problem.
To be badly under-rehearsed
given the deviant new script.

Picking oakum jolting you
from a comedy of errors
to the treadmill of verse.

A Paris finale. Wormwood.
Absinth that turns milky
when you add water.

Bratislava

Freedom from oppression
emptied boatloads of tourists

into the streets. Ferried
them past graffiti-spattered

art nouveau walls, avenues
of chestnuts, candelabrums

in pink and white. Restored
palaces in the town square.

Added a touch of whimsy:
a brass Napoleon leaning

on a seat, a workman
emerging from a manhole.

Filled a shop with Bohemian
glass, cut and engraved,

opaque or coloured, decanters,
vases, bowls in cobalt, ruby,

cranberry. Added a dash
of realpolitik at the door,

a muscled thug's frown
guarding too much freedom.

North wind

A north wind
opens the flywire door,
bangs it shut.
Hammers hard
at the roof.

Sand scuffs
the edges of the floor.
A wet towel
lies twisted, forgotten.

Sheets snarled
on the bed
tangle the imprint
of your absence.

I stand
in the doorway,
a visitor,
listening to the steady
heartbeat of waves.

Move outside.

Bark peels off a tree
like sunburnt skin.
I press my palm
into its trunk,
head bowed,
ants writing their story
across the back
of my hand.

Pieta

A mother's love
bearing the weight of her son.

The cruelty of contrast.
An aureole of innocence
crowning her head,
her long dark hair
falling across his nakedness.
Hiding his guilt, his anguish.
His body thin, ice
cold. Ice in his veins.
His flesh broken
on the cross of youth.
Nails driven in
by diffidence. His failure
to resist. The mob
howling for conformity.

The look on her face
close to rapture.
A devout forgiveness.
A recognition.

The Story Of A Life

comes down to this

silence between breaths
like the pause
when a conductor
points his baton at the orchestra
and the audience stirs

a nightdress soiled
with faded flowers

a photo by the bed
a young couple
from another age
their faces spinning with life
as if what lay ahead
had no beginning

words peeled off
like strips of wallpaper

a drawer full
of misplaced memories
a flower pressed
into a book of lost desire
calcified grief

an imprint on a mirror
a former self
smoothed in the rippled
mirth of youth

a hand stretched out
hoping to connect
with the coordinates of love

the body's last shudder
like a ferry
eased into a pier
has finally berthed

a wardrobe of coat hangers

Word

after W.S.Merwin's poem 'Air'

Already it's morning.
I'm pinned under its skin
wriggling. Wind
plucks at the strings of trees,
the hum of creation.

Will it blow hot, will it blow cold?

I remember shortcuts
that led to a maze of losses.
I remember the long road
that arrived
at a consonant, a vowel,
brevity of truth.

Birds stretched across the light
a feathered sentence,
the ocean rolling inside me
with its debris of words.

Litter of dross, litter of gold?

I forget the owl
I forget those pieces
I forced into the jigsaw
a wing away from wisdom
that buckled the page.
Left bruises.

Starting again, warmed
by this first sun. Walking
through a hole in the sky
smiling.

Forest

If you stray off the track
in pursuit of the lyrebird you heard,
segue of magpie/kookaburra/parrot,
brushing fronds from your face,
finding the bird's call
behind you instead of ahead,
black globular eyes
tracking you down,
you may experience a shudder
of panic as the forest
closes in. Mountain ash,
tree ferns, cockatoos sweeping the sky
inhale your presence.
Wind slaps strips of bark
against the trunks, tapping out
resined silence. Move into this stillness,
into this rhythm with your own song.
You are not lost,
you have found a part of yourself
as ancient as trees,
as luminous as words.

An Elegant Sufficiency

My mother's *Robert*
still clashes in my ears
like cymbals.
Makes me sit up straight.
Take my hands
out of my pockets.
Lift my elbows
off the table.
Makes me jump.

Manners would help
cover up my failings,
along with
elocution lessons.

It's not pitches, Robert,
it's pic-tures.
I repeated pic-tures
pic-tures all the way
to the pitches.

Don't say you're full
Robert, say you've had
an elegant sufficiency.
I tried it out
on a friend's parents.
The look on their faces
ensured I was full
from then on.

When I was her parent,
the scales tipped
by the weight of age
and illness,
my *Mum* made her jump
as much as her *Robert*.

So I understood
when, in the nursing home,
she said, *I'm always*
glad to see you, and I'm
glad when you leave.

She left, having had
an elegant sufficiency.

from *Caught Jesting*

2018

Capturing A Tram's Value

Finally the man
stopped shouting at someone
on his mobile phone.
I wanted to ask everyone
on the crowded tram
to applaud, but realised
nobody could bring
their hands together.

I was tempted to join in
the pungent flow
of the man's tirade. Wanted to suggest
we the captive audience
didn't need to know
that somebody's bottom line
needed tweaking, that this
was a game-changer,
a tough sell that involved
value capture. And if they both
were on the same page
why the argument
over getting rid of the office's
metamorphic furniture?
At the end of the day or otherwise.
And I needed clarification
about the facts of the matter.
If the furniture issue
was a no-brainer, how come
they were still arguing over it?
Was it the business deal
that was doable
or the boss's over-sexed wife?
And was the Director
involved in the car crash,
who sustained injuries
incompatible with living,
actually dead?

Real Men

In Queensland real men
wear shorts all the year round,
with no undies underneath.

A real man drove his wife
to a shopping centre.
By the time they spluttered
into the car park
the engine was playing up.
You do the shopping,
he said, *I'll fix the car.*

When she returned
she had to force her way
through a crowd
assembled round their vehicle.
Two legs stuck out
from under the chassis,
the male genitalia
on full display.
She knelt down,
gathered up the appendages
and shuffled them
back under the shorts
as best she could.
Stood up. Turned round.
Saw her husband
standing in the crowd.

The mechanic, another
real man, needed
three stitches in his head.

Mrs. Ned Kelly

I had a few too many
gins on our wedding night.
It was all a secret see.
He didn't want the troopers
after me. Thoughtful he was.
But I got a terrible fright
the next morning. Woke up
to find the bed sagging
to the floor and a monster
beside me. Face like a plough share.
Metal chest and legs.
I screamed. Is it any wonder
I'm still a virgin.

Mrs. Jack Ripper

He kept me in stitches, he did,
wiv his tall tales about girls
on the game, being carved up
and their guts spread
all over the place.
He made it all sound so real.
Gave me nightmares. But
you had to laugh. Cor,
what a cheeky little devil.

He worked as a butcher
in Whitechapel at the time.
Brought me home the choicest cuts.
But getting the blood out
of his aprons was more trouble
than it was werf.

He had some peculiar 'abits.
Very protective he was.
Wouldn't let me read
the papers. Cor, what he made up
was worse than anyfing
they printed. *Don't want you
getting upset Lil,* he'd say.
Well I mean, you had to laugh.

Then all of a sudden
he insists we was moving.
To Bognor of all places.
He got a job in the 'ospital
clearing up the gory bits
after the operations.
He even got to help out
in some nasty amputations.
So he said. Cor, the stories
he came home wiv. Laugh?

The Way To Gay Love

1.
save the mincing for the kitchen

2.
barrack for his football team
even if it is Collingwood

3.
when fondling his buns
do not accuse him
of resorting to implants

4.
never wear matching Lycra
when out cycling

5.
make friends with his mother
if just to borrow her recipes

6.
if you agree to an open relationship
don't text all your friends
they'll only join his queue

7.
a bowl full of lube and condoms
surrounded by thick phallic candles
African violets
and a portrait of Mary and baby Jesus
may not be all that romantic

8.
don't bitch when he kisses
the Lhaso Apso Alsatian cross
the way he kisses you

9.
resist squeezing your hand
between his thighs
in front of his RSL President father

10.
stop passing on his drugs
to your mother

11.
don't raise the cut/uncut debate
during a barbecue
especially if it features offal

12.
when he's on his knees
don't assume
he is about to propose

13.
when he tells you it's over
refrain from the threat
of tossing yourself off the Bolte Bridge
wearing a black wedding dress
and clutching a crucifix

14.
finally
stop pinching his drugs back
from your mother

In The Bar

Because summer
has overreached itself
and spread into March,
we sit outside in the courtyard
at the back of Margot's
sipping red wine.
Dr. Michael Mosley will tell us
it's good for us. As we tell ourselves.

After snatching at passing plates
of chicken sandwiches
in the bridal garden of friends,
we are in need of food.
We order a vegetarian platter
and a pizza to share.

We've just been to our second
gay wedding in a week,
I tell the waiter, who's new
to us. *All four husbands*
are in their seventies, like us.
What wedding presents
do you give to men our age?
A pair of racing Zimmer frames?
A tube of KY and a defibrillator?
A matching set of floral
continence pads? He laughs.
Gives me a look. As if to say,
'Despite your age I'll have to keep
an eye on you, just in case'.
And off he goes to place our order.

Body Parts

Head over heels in love
I paraded arm in arm
with my new amour
in front of my ex-lover,
whose nose, twitching,
was clearly out of joint.
Suffering foot-and-mouth
disease, his ham-fisted
abuse, a knee-jerk reaction,
proved we'd never see
eye to eye on our divorce.

I worked hard at this
new affair. Kept my nose
to the grindstone, toed
the line, my finger always
on the pulse, waiting
on him hand and foot.

Then he left me. I was
glad really, he'd cost me
an arm and a leg.

Man In A Glass Suit

'The delight and strength of these poems lie in the unique quality of
the voice … the depth of sorrow and the height of hilarity are shaped
and presented, with breathtaking precision …'
Carmel Bird

'Some of these poems will grab at your heart, others will fuel your
angst but all will remind you of the humanity we share and the fun
there is to be had with words.'
E.A.Gleeson

An Elegant Sufficiency

'I'm drawn to the attractive scope, humanity and acuity of Wallis's
vision. His poems reflect wide travel in fact and in imagination …'
Michael Sharkey

'Rob Wallis's poetry will immediately charm you with it's sure-footed
and literate wit. But this is just a ruse – it's real agenda, barely hidden,
is to haunt you with its perceptive observations and acute tenderness.'
Andy Jackson

Caught Jesting

'These poems are brim-full of wit, word-play and piss-taking views in
verse … he writes feelingly hilarious accounts of gay love … This is a
hearty book of clever musings and endless, knockabout mischief.'
Philip Salom

'Rob's wordplay is a hoot. The collection strikes a balance between
cheeky and curmudgeonly that will hit the spot for (frankly) anyone
over a certain age … It had me laughing from the getgo.'
Robyn Annear

i

www.ingramcontent.com/pod-product-compliance
Lightning Source LLC
Chambersburg PA
CBHW051211090426

42740CB00022B/3464